Lesbian Sex Stories
By Marcy Mink

There were five people jammed into Tori's little red Honda and everyone was drunk except for her. That was usual for a Friday night, but they weren't usually in this part of town. If it weren't for Jo volunteering them to pick Shauna up after work, she wouldn't be here at all under any circumstances.

"Where the hell is this place?" Tori asked, as she cruised along the street called Broadway on the map and the pussy mile on campus.

"Shauna said you couldn't miss it," Veronica Goings offered.

"Yeah, well, this is our third time up the street. If we don't find it soon, I'm heading back to the dorm."

"Don't be a stick in the mud, Tori, we'll find it," Candice Ford replied.

"Yeah, take a hit of this and chill out," Joann Taylor said, passing a blunt to the front seat.

Joann was her best friend. They had known each other since grade school and roomed together in the upperclassman dorm. They were thinking about getting an apartment after this semester and she knew Tori didn't smoke. Tori should have been mad, but she wasn't. Jo was like that, always pushing her to relax and as she put it, "live a little."

"Get that shit away from me," Tori snarled as Monica Riley tried to pass her the joint.

Monica inhaled deeply and blew out a cloud of the reeking smoke right into Tori's face.

The car exploded into a fit of giggles as Tori coughed and choked. She desperately wanted to roll down a window, but in this area of town her innate caution overcame her desire.

Hookers ranged up and down the sidewalks, many accompanied by their pimps. Strip clubs and adult book stores decorated the rundown facades in garish neon light. College students prowled along in groups, egging each other on and getting drunk. The occasional beat cop and his partner could be seen, as well as a few black and whites parked in warehouse loading docks. Hotels advertised rooms by the hour with free XXX feeds. Dealers had their corners staked out and junkies could be seen in every possible recess.

"There it is," Veronica said, pointing to a rundown building with a 'girls girls girls' sign flashing in red and gold.

A larger sign proclaimed The Harem in red lettering, but the sign was almost burned out with only the small 'a' still lit, explaining how they had missed it.

Tori rarely drank and never used drugs. She was the straight arrow among her friends. Her slightly prudish demeanor was tolerated because she was Jo's best friend and because she didn't mind being designated driver. She had a contact high now and found parking to be difficult in the narrow alley behind the place. The lines seemed uneven, but she wasn't sure if that was just bad city planning or the way her head was spinning.

They all piled out and made their way to the front, stepping through a doorway covered only by Persian beads. Inside the door was a small foyer with Arabic murals and some very explicit photos of the dancers. A small, greasy man in black leathers sat behind a bank teller style grill with a money box.

"Ten dollar cover, two drink minimum," he declared, apparently unfazed by their gender.

After they paid, they made their way into a large, open room, with a main stage in the middle and two smaller stages at each end. The décor was a pathetic attempt at an Arabian harem, with pillows and silk wall hangings. Plastic scimitars hung on the walls and the waitresses all wore gauzy pants and pointy-toed slippers that reminded her of Jeannie from the old TV show. Each table had a small candle burning on it. The place reeked of marijuana and stale beer.

It wasn't very crowded and they found a table near the main stage. A few of the male customers gave them curious looks. One table had a bunch of frat rats and they seemed to be paying them more attention than the other patrons.

Tori had the idea they were egging each other on to see if the girls wanted company, but nothing came of it. Soon a topless barmaid appeared.

She was an older woman, with sad, tired eyes and a listless manner that bespoke of extreme exhaustion. Tori noticed her breasts were large and very firm, obviously implants.

"What can I get you?" she asked.

Everyone ordered exotic sounding drinks, except for Tori. She was still flying from the weed and wanted to try and clear her head.

"Do you have coffee?" she asked.

"Ignore her," Candice said, before the

woman could answer.

"Yeah, bring her a pink panty pulldown," Monica cackled.

"I don't..."

"Be cool, Tor. It's only two drinks and we're staying till Shauna gets off. You'll be plenty sober by then," Joann said reasonably.

"Sweetie?" the woman asked, with a tired, but apparently genuine smile.

Normally, she would have demurred, but she was feeling strange from the weed and she couldn't really make sense of her thoughts.

"All right, I guess," she said.

"So, when's Shauna gonna be on stage?" Veronica asked excitedly.

"Probably be a while, they work in rotations. She'll get a main stage introduction, then work the side stages, then the floor, then a break, then main stage again," Joann said.

"You sure seem to know a lot about strip clubs," Monica observed.

"I worked at T & A's two months last summer to pay for the cruise."

"Really? Make a lot?" the perpetually broke Veronica asked.

"Oh, yeah. It's really good money if you have a body or can dance. Even better if you will work the back room."

"The back room?" Tori asked.

"Yeah. Girls take guys to the back rooms for private dances. If all you do is dance, it's thirty bucks, half going to the house, but if you're willing to give him a hand job or blow, you can make a mint because the house only takes ten more for extra services, no matter how much you make."

"So, did you blow a lot of cute guys?" Monica asked.

She was a great person when sober, but when she started drinking she became really mean and snide. Everyone was used to it, so Joann took no offense.

"No, I was making over two hundred a night in tips. I didn't need to run any extra risks."

"Two hundred a night? I was wondering why Shauna was doing this," Veronica exclaimed.

"She wants that Mercedes pretty bad, but Mommy and Daddy are in a snit because her grades sucked so they won't get it for her."

"How much do the waitresses make?" Tori asked.

"Not much. They're usually older women and don't look all that good anymore. A lot are single moms. These places rack up most of their profit on the weekends. The big earners usually only work two nights a week, so most of the waitresses you see on Friday and Saturday night are the dancers Monday through Thursday."

"That sucks."

"Yeah, it's a double dose of shit. They have to wait tables on the busy nights and when they are working there are fewer patrons so fewer tips."

"Why do they put up with it?" Candice asked.

"Most of them don't have any other option. I mean, it's one thing for me or Shauna to do it for a short while to get some extra cash. It's another thing entirely when your family depends on you doing it. It's fun and exciting and all that for a while, but the only reason it's like that is because we can walk away anytime we choose. It's a pretty crappy job when it's all you have."

"Think Shauna will rack up, she has pretty big boobs," Candice asked.

"No, she'll do all right, but she hasn't got the mentality to really make money at it," Jo said thoughtfully.

"What do you mean?"

"The trick to it is to make every guy thinks you're interested in him. You hook 'em, then lead them on through the night. Shauna might do that with a cute guy, but she won't do it with every guy. The cute ones are usually the ones with the least money, they are guys who count on looks to get them in with women. You want to make money, you make nice with the dorks and geeks and losers. The poor bastards couldn't hope to get your attention in a bar or at a party. Once you smile at one, he'll follow you like a puppy, tipping heavily, ponying up for table and private dances, maybe you come out on break and sit with him, let him buy you a drink or two, whatever."

"That sounds so cold blooded," Tori said.

"It's like any other business, Tor, you're here to part the customer from his cash," Jo said.

Tori was flying now, the smoke in the club was at least half reefer and she was having trouble marshalling her chaotic thoughts. When the waitress returned and served their drinks, she fished into her pocket on impulse and dropped a twenty dollar bill on her tray.

"I don't have change, sweetie, you have to go to the bartender to get ones."

Tori colored and stammered as the others laughed like a pack of hyenas.

"She didn't want change, she was just giving you a big tip," Joann said with a smile on her face.

"Thank you," the woman said with an obviously heartfelt smile.

"You're welcome," Tori managed.

"Be careful with that," Joann warned after the waitress had moved out of earshot.

"Careful?" Tori asked.

"Yeah. I know you're just a sweetheart and were trying to be nice, but this is a cutthroat business, like I said before. Word gets around fast. Big spenders are always given special attention and I don't think you want that."

The house lights dimmed and a spot lit the stage. A DJ's voice boomed over the PA system.

"Ladies and gentlemen, all the way from El Paso, Texas, put your hands together for Lilith!"

A dark haired girl in white cowgirl boots, a little white Stetson, tight short shorts and a white vest with red fringe came out on stage as everyone clapped. She had long legs and a big chest, which the vest barely concealed. Tori thought she was a little older than herself and pretty, though by no means a knockout.

Tori sipped her drink, finding it to be very fruity and not as harsh as many drinks she had tried. The girl did a slow strip tease and guys came up, stuffing bills into her red g-string. Monica ran up waving a bill and did the same as everyone at the table cheered. Before her dance was done, all of the girls had given her a dollar except Tori. Try as they might, the others couldn't convince her to do so, even when the girl smiled invitingly and stood still for a moment at the end of the stage.

When she finished, she gathered her clothes, took a bow and, as Joann had predicted, moved down to the stage at one end of the place. A few guys followed her to that stage, predominantly the ones she had danced close to while on center stage.

"Jeeze, Tor, you could have at least given her a buck," Joann said.

"Yeah, get with the program," Candice added.

"Now she thinks you didn't like her," Monica said.

"It's not that!" Tori exclaimed.

Before they could do more than laugh, the DJ's voice came back on.

"And now, from way up north, we bring you, Bunny! Give her a big hand."

She was blonde and tanned, with a massive bust and wide hips. She wore faux fur stiletto boots, lederhosen and a little white top, with a ski cap. As she danced, Tori was mildly aroused. That was embarrassing, but no one seemed to notice. She didn't tip this one either and soon she gave way to another girl.

After that one, the DJ called again.

"Ladies and gentlemen, from the Caribbean and performing for the first time on stage, put your hands together for Chiquita!"

Everyone at the table went wild cheering when Shauna came out. She had her hair up and dressed with tropical fruit and wore a tiny halter top and a long skirt with a slit up to her hip. As she danced they kept up a steady stream from their table to the stage, stuffing her g-string with bills and laughing. Even Tori managed to get up the nerve to go up several times.

When she finished, she was gathering up her things when the DJ called again.

"That was Chiquita, ladies and gentlemen. Don't forget our two for one beer specials and remember to tip your waitress. Lilith is now available for table dances, so guys, get those bills out. Our next dancer is fresh off the reservation. Put your hands together for Comanche!"

Everyone was starting to rise to follow Shauna down to the smaller stage, but when Comanche stepped on stage, Tori found herself stuck fast in her chair.

Her hair was long, braided with a feather and reached down to the small of her back. Large, full breasts were held back by a faux buckskin bikini top. Unlike the first performers, they were in perfect proportion to her wide shoulders and hips. Her legs were long and sleek, the short, triangular buckskin skirt barely hiding them.

Instead of the high heels most of the girls wore, she wore moccasins that laced up and covered most of her calves.

Her face was classically beautiful, with high cheekbones and forehead, sensuous lips and an aquiline nose, but her eyes really held Tori. They were brown, intelligent and unbelievably intense as they scanned the crowd. They stopped on her table and the girl smiled.

"Come on, Tori," Monica called as she and Candice and Veronica walked off.

"Beautiful, isn't she?" Joann said in a quiet voice.

"She's incredible," Tori mouthed.

"Wait till you see her in action."

The music started and she moved sensuously about the stage. She didn't seem to be a trained dancer, so much as naturally graceful and fluid of motion. Her copper skin glistened under the light and Tori felt the room get hot and stuffy. She had always kept her attraction to a certain kind of girl well hidden, but now it was all she could do not to drool.

When Comanche turned her back and undid the clasp on her top, Tori felt her breath catch in her throat. Comanche turned back, holding the garment over her breasts and danced a moment longer before tossing it off stage. The guys all cheered and clapped, but Tori was oblivious to it.

The girl's breasts were incredible. They were proud and firm, capped with large areolas and thick nipples. Tori couldn't seem to take her eyes off of them. They swayed and bounced gently as Comanche danced. Tori was so enthralled she didn't even hear Joann speaking. It was just a minor buzz in the background.

When the dancer bent over and slowly pushed her skirt down, Tori felt like she had been kicked in the stomach. She couldn't seem to breathe at all as the soft expanse of the girl's beautiful ass was revealed. She wore only a tiny black g-string and Tori could easily see where it clung to her fat mound.

The girl stepped out of her skirt and began to move slowly around the stage, holding her g-string out for guys to stuff bills in, or presenting her ass, which they all took the opportunity to run their hands over. Tori was barely cognizant of Joann stuffing a bill into her hand. When she noticed it she blushed crimson and stared at the floor.

"Go ahead, Tor, you know you want to," her friend encouraged.

Tori stood hesitantly and walked mechanically toward the stage. She felt like every eye in the place was on her and she nearly fell when her feet moved from the carpet to the tile surrounding the stage. When she looked back up, Comanche was staring at her and Tori felt her face flush.

As Tori approached, Comanche moved to the end of the stage and gracefully squatted down. She spread her long legs and hooked both thumbs into her g-string, pulling it outward. Tori could clearly see her thick black pubes and the coral colored lips peeking out as she shakily placed the bill inside.

"Thank you," she whispered in a seductive voice that somehow drowned out the music and cat calls.

"Y..y...your welcome," Tori stammered.

The girl smiled and winked before rising in a fluid motion and gathering her things. Tori made her way back to her seat and sat down.

"You look like you've just seen a ghost," Joann said with a smile.

"I..."

"Shhh. Don't say anything. You aren't a good liar and you can't lie to me even if you were, I know you too well."

Tori wondered what she was talking about, but let it pass as the others came back by.

"What are you two doing?" Veronica asked.

"Holding our table. Place is filling up and if we leave, we won't get it back," Joann said quickly.

"Oh, cool," she replied as they breezed down to the other stage.

Joann crammed another bill into Tori's hand.

"Go on, Tor. She's at the other stage."

"Jo, I..."

"Shush. Take your drink for some courage, but get moving, the song's already starting."

"Ladies and gentlemen," the DJ called, "Direct your attention center stage for our featured performer, Pinky Pumpkins!"

A roar went up from the crowd and most of the patrons crowded towards the center stage. Tori ignored them, ignored everything as she gulped down the last of her drink and took a seat by the smaller stage. She was the only one on this end of the club as Comanche glided out from behind the curtain.

She was still wearing only her g-string and moccasins. Tori couldn't believe how toned her body was or how beautiful. She was just staring when the girl smiled directly at her and began to dance. This song was different than the one she had performed to center stage, it was more frenetic and allowed her to show off her strength and stamina rather than accentuating her grace. When she held the hips of an imaginary lover and bucked her hips as if fucking her, Tori thought she would die.

Comanche whirled and twirled, working up a good sweat that bathed her skin and caused the light to glitter of the soft curves of her body. The music slowed suddenly, and became soft as it flowed into a sensual acoustic interlude. Comanche fell to her stomach a little to Tori's left and then rolled over twice, so she was lying on her tummy with her feet pressed against the gilt work rail at the edge of the stage. She pushed up, in a single languid motion, spreading her legs and raising her ass, while pressing back.

Her pussy was directly in front of Tori, only inches from her face. She knew it had to be her imagination, but she swore she could smell the delicate aroma of the dancer's arousal.

Comanche had her torso flat on stage, but she glanced back and pulled her g-string to one side, leaving her pussy bare.

Her mound was fat and fleshy, but the lips were delicately formed and gaped open just enough to reveal the darker pink of her inner folds. Her pubic thatch was strange, seemingly starting from a central line and growing outwards. The heady scent of her arousal and exertions was now obvious.

"Thanks for sticking with me, I hate going before the feature act," she said in an exotic whisper.

Tori wanted to reply. She desperately wanted to say something, but her tongue seemed cloven to her palate. The girl smiled, rolled over so she was sitting with her legs still spread and thrust her pelvis towards Tori.

"You're a shy one, I like that. If you want to tip me better do it now, the song's almost over."

Tori nodded mutely and extended her hand with the bill Joan had given her. Comanche glanced left and right, then dropped to her back. With one hand she grabbed her g-string and pulled it aside. With the other, she grabbed Tori's wrist and guided the shaking girl's hand to her pussy.

"Thanks, babe," Comanche said as the song ended.

She sat up quickly, pecked Tori on the forehead and was gone. Tori wandered back towards their table totally lost. She could feel the girl's wetness on her fingertips, but was unsure if it was sweat or something else. She absently held her fingers to her nose and the heady scent left no doubts. She drifted past the table and down towards the other stage, oblivious to her friends calling her.

Several patrons had gathered around, but Tori still got a seat at the middle of the small stage. She dug another bill out of her pocket and waited tensely.

"Ladies and gentleman, that was Pinky Pumpkins! She'll be back in half an hour. Right now we have Boobarella center stage. Camille and Comanche

are on the side stages and Bunny, Lilith and our new girl, Chiquita are available for table dances. If you really want a treat, remember to ask about the private dances, only thirty bucks for three songs, until midnight."
Comanche came out and while she smiled at all of the men around, she gave Tori a wink before she began to bump and grind to an old Motown hit. Tori was watching, spellbound when Comanche passed very close to her.

"Tilt your head back," she whispered.

Tori didn't even think not to and she was stunned when the girl leaned forward and rested her tits on either side of Tori's head and shook them. They were so soft and the skin was so silky, Tori felt a contraction in her deep muscles. It was only then that she realized how aroused she was. Her nipples were poking out and she could feel her pussy twitching.

Comanche was looking down at her and Tori colored furiously at she men hooted and made cat calls.

"Stand up and put a dollar in your mouth," the girl whispered.

Tori did so, feeling foolish, but not caring. Her blood was pounding in her temples as Comanche reached back and grasped the gold pole that stood upright through the stage. Her hips were right in front of Tori's face and they sensuously undulated. Comanche smiled, leaned back up and caught the back of Tori's head with one hand, while pulling her g-string aside with the other. She pulled Tori's head between her thighs, until the bill was lying flat against her skin. As the song ended, she let the g-string snap back, trapping the dollar.

"Thank you," she cooed, before collecting the few bills on stage and darting back behind the curtain after a quick bow.

Tori could feel the men staring and pointing, but she floated back to their table without her feet ever once hitting the floor. At least, that's how it felt. She had barely sat down when the waitress showed up.

"Can I get you girls another?" she asked.

Tori nodded while the others placed orders. She noticed Joann ordered a diet coke and again wondered about her friend's strange behavior. Jo usually drank them all under the table. When the waitress returned with the drinks, she took everyone's second ticket, but when Tori tried to hand hers over, the blonde just shook her head slightly.

"Keep it, honey. I go off in ten and you can use it to get something from Tara," she whispered.

"Well, seems like you're making a lot of friends," Monica said.

"Monica, stow it," Jo said.

Jo's voice was soft, but it carried that deadly edge Tori recognized as the calm before the storm. The dark haired girl was taken aback, but managed to laugh it off.

"Sure, sure, I was just joking."

"No, you were being a bitch."

"Jeeze, calm down, I was..."

"You were being a bitch," Jo said in that flat tone.

"Well, excuuuuse me!"

Tori was afraid there was about to be a fight. She pitied Monica if there was. Jo would kick her ass soundly, of that she was certain.

"Jesus H. Christ, we're here to have fun. Knock it off, both of you," Candice shouted.

Jo smiled and took a sip of her coke while Monica managed not to put her foot in her mouth and let it go.

Tori barley noticed the next two girls on stage. She was in her own little world as Shauna came over and plopped down in Jo's lap.

"What did you think?" she asked excitedly.

"Great! How much did you make?" Veronica asked.

"Almost fifty, but at least half of it was

from you guys," she said, taking a swig of Jo's coke.

She stayed and they all talked while a girl named Raquel danced on the stage. As the song was ending she stood up.

"Gotta get to work, be back later," she said as she hurried over to a guy waving to her.

"Ladies and gentlemen, on center stage it's Strawberry. Dixie and Raquel are on the side stages and all of our girls are available for table and private dances. Two for one beer specials are available at the rear bar or through your waitress and remember to tip these girls."

A new waitress came by and everyone

ordered drinks. Tori wasn't paying a lot of attention to the girl on stage, a trim black girl with fire engine red hair. She was half watching Bunny, bumping and grinding in a big black man's lap and half watching Strawberry when Comanche suddenly plopped down in her lap.

She had changed outfits, now sporting a blue satin bra and blue micro mini with matching stockings and black stiletto heels. Having this incredibly sexy girl in sitting in her lap was the strongest sexual thrill she had ever known. It would have been perfect, except for the laughter and comments of her friends.

"Feel like a dance?" she purred in Tori's ear.

Tori was shocked, embarrassed as could be and utterly at a loss. The others were all laughing, and urging her to do it.

"How much for a private dance?" Jo asked.

"Thirty bucks for three songs."

"Come on, everybody kick in," the tall girl said, tossing a twenty on the table.

The others quickly tossed bills in the pile and Tori felt herself flush, though she wasn't sure it was all embarrassment.

Comanche scooped up the bills, stuffed them in her bra and stood up. Grabbing

Tori's hand she led the nearly petrified girl back past a grinning bouncer. Comanche held her hand firmly while trying the first two doors they passed, the third one opened and Comanche stepped in, pulling Tori along behind her.

The room was painted a dark green and lit with subtle lighting. Tori was astounded to see one wall was composed of a two way mirror that looked out on the main room from behind the center stage. Comanche gently pushed Tori down into the single furnishing, an overstuffed chair.

The music from out front was being piped in over speakers concealed in the floor.

"Get ready, baby, I'm going to knock your socks off," Comanche said as the song faded and another began.

She locked eyes with Tori and her hips began to sway to the music. Tori couldn't move as she watched Comanche remove her top, letting her breasts bounce free. She moved closer and turned, bending at the waist as she pushed the short skirt down. Tori wanted so badly to touch that silky expanse of golden skin, but she was too afraid to move.

Comanche stood, turned around, placed her hand on her hip and cocked her head.

"I come in here ten times a night usually, with guys that make my skin crawl. I don't begrudge them their little fancies, but I finally come in here with a cute little fox and you sit there like a statue. What gives?"

"I don't know what I can do," Tori said at last.

"Whatever I decide you can," Comanche laughed.

She put a knee on either side of Tori's hips and slid into the chair, until their pelvises were pressed together. When Tori didn't move, the tall girl placed her hands on Tori's wrists and gently guided them to her behind.

Tori was still unsure, but her hands seemed to know what they were doing as she stroked and squeezed the soft, yet resilient skin of Comanche's ass.

"Yessssss," the girl hissed in Tori's ear.

Her hips were working in time to the music, and her breasts were pressed into Tori's. She had her head down and was nibbling on Tori's neck. She sat up quickly and again looked into Tori's eyes.

Tori couldn't break eye contact. She saw amusement in those eyes, but also compassion or concern or something. It was so hard to think.

"You're like a kitten," she said softly.

"Kitten?"

"Yeah. Soft, small, curious but scared

and so very cute."

Tori blushed. This whole evening had been so strange and now she couldn't tell if she was being complimented or insulted. The drinks and grass obviously had something to do with her state, but she knew this beautiful girl's attention would have rattled her wits even without them.

"Well, kittens love milk, so lets try this," Comanche said, catching one of her breasts and guiding the nipple to Tori's lips. She gently rubbed the hardened nipple over Tori's lips. Tori was beside herself. She didn't know what to do. All of her secret fantasies and even her imaginings from her reading hadn't prepared her for the moment when she could act on them.

"Come on, all babies love nipples. You look hungry and Mommy's here with your dinner."

Tori shuddered as her desire spiked wildly. She hesitantly parted her lips and Comanche pressed her torso forward, pushing her nipple and areola into Tori's mouth.

"Mmmm," she growled, when Tori cautiously rolled her tongue around that thick, golden nipple.

Her skin was salty, but sweet and it just got sweeter as Tori pulled at the nipple in her mouth. Her hands were still stroking the soft skin of Comanche's ass as the girl rotated her hips in Tori's lap. She could have just stayed there forever, but Comanche pulled back. The nipple leaving Tori's mouth made an incredibly sexy popping sound.

Tori looked up at the girl quizzically, causing her to laugh.

"Other one is feeling neglected," she said in that sexy whisper, before guiding it to Tori's lips.

This time they parted unhesitantly and she greedily sucked, rolling the nipple and puckered areola under her tongue as she sucked.

Time lost all meaning as her world shrunk down to just her and the soft, salty, sexy girl in her lap. Comanche's mound, bumping and rubbing against

Tori's pussy was driving her crazy. She barely noticed when the girl sat back and slowed her pace.

"Just about out of time, kitten. Be a good little girl help mummy get those jeans down."

Comanche's hands were already working on her fly as she was speaking and the only help she needed was Tori raising her ass. Comanche left the jeans around Tori's ankles and slid back into her lap. She pushed her hand between their bodies, burrowing under the waistband and into the steamy confines of Tori's red panties.

Comanche expertly found her entrance and curled two fingers into her tight passage. Tori was so wet she experienced no pain, only a wild thrill. Comanche pressed her mound to her wrist and began that rolling motion Tori has so loved earlier. Except now, with each stab forward Comanche drove her fingers into Tori's molten sex.

Two thrusts and Tori was moaning. In ten she was biting her lip and fighting back the rising tide. Comanche seemed to be taking her cue from the driving rhythm of the music. Somewhere between halfbeats, Tori's body stiffened and on the downbeat she felt her pussy quiver in delight.

Pure bliss raced through her system like a runaway freight train and slammed into her mind in an explosion of sparks. She saw starbursts and heard a rushing wave like the ocean in her ears as the pleasure carried her away. Her cry of pleasure was eclipsed by the shriek of a guitar and the pounding blast of the drums as the musicians reached their crescendo.

Comanche slid down her body, pushing her legs wide. She wrapped one hand around Tori's thigh and used it to pull her pussy open. Tori opened her eyes in time to see Comanche push her nose into Tori's pubes. At the first contact of her tongue on Tori's exposed clit, she came again.

It was unreal, the explosions of pleasure from her pussy coming again and again, seemingly timed to match each swipe of that silken tongue over her clit. Her back arched, she whimpered and found it impossible to breathe as her body convulsed again and again. When she felt a long finger slide into her passage another blast of unreal euphoria tore through her already quivering body. Again and again and again the waves of pleasure assailed her mind, until she lost all connection with reality. She was totally absorbed in it, oblivious to all else.

When she regained some semblance of reason, she found Comanche already had her top and skirt back on. The dark headed girl helped her to her feet and watched in amusement as Tori tried to get her pants refastened.

"Thanks babe," she said, taking Tori's face in her hands.

Comanche kissed her then, not a peck but a deep, tongue swirling, toe curling soul kiss. When it broke, she opened the door and escorted Tori back to the main room.

Tori's legs were like rubber bands and she stumbled towards the table. Jo was at her side instantly, with a strong arm around her waist.

"Must have been some dance," Veronica laughed.

"You okay, Tor?" Jo asked, the concern in her voice cutting off further comments.

"I'm a little dizzy," she managed.

"Gimme the keys," Jo said theatrically.

Tori looked into her friends eyes and knew with certainty that Jo knew. She knew, too that Jo was covering for her, giving her the out of letting the drinks explain her flushed face and disorientation. As she handed them over, a secret smile passed between them. The kind that only the most intimate friends ever shared.

"Waitress, another round!" Monica hollered.

"Yeah, Tori's getting blasted!" Veronica enthused.

Tori decided she couldn't fight it, so she gulped down another drink as her friends egged her on. It would be okay. Jo would look after her.

***

"Oh god, please," Tori groaned after another round of dry heaves passed.

Jo laughed as she picked her smaller friend up and deposited her in the shower. Jo turned the taps on hot and closed the curtain. Tori groaned as the hot water hit her skin and feebly tried to crawl out of the shower. She gave up when her stomach lurched and just laid down at the back of the stall.

After several minutes, her stomach calmed somewhat and the pounding in her ears subsided to a dull throb. Jo helped her out and dried her off with a big fuzzy towel. Tori was used to Saturday mornings doing this, but she was used to being on the other side of the towel.

Back in the room, Jo had coffee made and Tori managed to choke down some ramen noodles. She slept most of the day and when she awoke, the room was dark and still. Jo was sitting at her desk with only the computer screen casting a weak glow on her face.

"How do you feel?" she asked when she realized Tori was awake.

"Awful. I won't ever do that again."

Jo laughed softly while closing her laptop down.

"We all say that. Hopefully, you'll be like the rest of us and break the vow before too long."

"I don't think so," Tori said, feeling her stomach lurch when she tried to sit up.

"Best get a move on, we're already late for the party at the Alpha house."

"Take my keys. I'm not up for anything right now."

"Ya sure?"

"Yeah, I'm sure."

Jo was watching her and Tori felt herself blush. She knew something needed to be said about last night, but words failed her. She knew Jo knew and she regretted not telling her sooner. Best friends didn't keep such secrets from each other.

"Jo, I..."

"Don't."

"Don't what?"

"Don't tell me you're a dyke. I know you feel the need to, but don't. It's all good."

"You sure? I mean..."

"Let it drop please," Jo said, standing quickly and grabbing Tori's keys.

"All right," she whispered as her friend breezed out of the room.

Tori cried then. The hurt in Jo's voice and posture had been so evident. She felt terrible, but had no clue how to fix things.

***

Jo stayed out Saturday night and all of Sunday. She came in long after Tori had fallen asleep and left before the crack of dawn. Tori spent all day trying to figure out how to make things right. She finally decided she would have to brave the storm and say her piece, even if Jo tried to stop her. It was a daunting prospect, but when she saw the light was on in the room when she got in from her late lab she was determined to do it.

"Jo, I..." she began as she opened the door to her room and walked in.

When she saw Comanche sitting there with Jo, she froze. Jo laughed, stood up and walked out the door. She paused in the hall and looked back in.

"You two have fun, fuck, whatever. I'll stay out till you give me a ring," she said before pecking Tori on the cheek and firmly closing the door.

Tori just stood there until the silence became awkward.

"You might as well sit down, Kitten," Comanche said in that same soft voice she had used in the private room.

"What's going on?" Tori managed.

"Well, it's a long story. Can I get you a beer? Or better yet some wine? I brought a bottle of Chardonnay. Jo said that's your favorite."

Comanche rose and turned her back on Tori, taking a chilled bottle out of the small fridge she and Jo shared.

"How do you know Jo? I'm so confused."

"I met Jo in her freshman year. I was TAing one of her classes."

"You're a student?" Tori asked incredulously.

Despite her confusion, she could feel tendrils of desire coiling in her tummy as she watched Comanche moving. It wasn't the calculated eroticism of a dancer, just a naturally sinuous and fluid motion, but when paired with such a gorgeous body, it was highly erotic.

"Grad student. Working on my masters in social anthropology, with an emphasis on Native American customs and religion."

"Why do you work at a strip club then?"

"I do come from a reservation," she said as she sat back down and handed Tori a glass of wine, "that isn't bullshit for the crowd."

She took a swallow of her beer before continuing. Her eyes locked with Tori's.

"It pays good, for one thing. For another, it's a night job and I make more two nights a week there than I would at any other job in town. I've got a grant, but it leaves very little to live on, much less money to send home every month to help my folks out. I've got three sisters and they're all sharp as tacks, but finding the money to send them to college is tough for my folks, so I get by on my grant money and send what I earn back to them for the girl's college funds."

"Oh."

"Surprised?" she asked with an enigmatic smile.

"Why didn't Jo act like she knew you?" Tori asked, not feeling comfortable answering the question.

"Well, Jo knows I'm a dyke. I put a move on her before she told me she didn't swing that way. Embarrassing, to say the least. We laugh about it now though. She knows my steady graduated and took up with some guy in Hollywood who promised to help her advance her acting career. I'm pretty sure he'll get her into porn and I hope she chokes on all that dick." she said vehemently.

When she noticed how Tori flinched, Comanche blushed.

"Sorry. I guess you can tell I'm still hurt, huh? Anyways, I've been down in the dumps and Jo was worried about me. She was also upset that Shauna was considering dancing. That girl ain't the brightest bulb in the chandelier and Jo was worried she would end up at one of the real dives. So when Shauna decided she was going to go through with it, Jo asked me to put in a good word for her with Maurice. No sweat, he's always looking for new girls and I picked up a fifty buck bonus when she started work. Arabia ain't the best club in town, but Maurice is retired and just runs it for something to do, so he isn't out to fuck anyone over and he's a nice old fellow. Kinda gets sweet on his girls and looks after us well."

"All right, but that still doesn't explain..."

"Patience, kitten, I'm coming to that. In between worrying about me and worrying about Shauna, Jo's been worrying about you."

"Me? But why?"

"You don't go out. You don't date. You're depressed a lot. She's a really great friend and she really cares about you."

"I know."

"So she started to wonder if you were les or bi and just afraid to approach anyone. She found your stash, by the way."

"Oh my god," Tori exclaimed, blushing beet red.

"I'm her only dyke friend, so of course she came to me for advice. I'm not going to lie to you, after she told me all about you and showed me some pictures, I was determined to meet you, but things just never worked out. Jo was afraid I was too hard assed for you."

Tori was still blushing, imagining Jo going through her collection of lesbian books. She thought she kept them in a safe place, but apparently not. Especially embarrassing was the knowledge that the bindings would fall open to her favorite passages in most of them.

"That changed when she saw some of your porn," she said, grinning when Tori shook her head.

"She still wasn't sure though, so we came up with getting you to the club. If you showed an interest, great, it was up to me to land you. If not, no embarrassment for Jo or hurt for me or you." "So if I hadn't shown an interest?"

"We wouldn't have even met, except for maybe me trying to get you to get a table dance. Of course Jo was going to pay for a private dance when I did, that was part of the plan."

"That stinker!"

"Go easy on her. If you aren't interested, I'll walk. She's just your best friend and she was a little hurt you had never told her. I told her just a few minutes ago you were cherry, probably having a lot of issues with it, so she felt better."

"I'm not angry. I love her even more for introducing us, even if it was sneaky."

"I'm glad to hear you say that. You're hotter than hell, but damn, you sure made me work for it."

"I've never been so nervous," Tori admitted.

"You're cute when you're nervous and shy is very sexy on you. It was all I could do not to throw you over my shoulder and take you home."

"I wish you had."

"Well, don't know you well enough to do my Conan routine on you," she said with a smile.

Tori didn't know what to say to that. For a long while they just sipped their drinks and looked at one another.

"Now what?" Tori asked.

"Depends on you, Kitten. I won't lie, I'd love to get into your pants, but I'm not too caught up in sex. If you need time, we can go slow. I'd like to date you, not just be fuck buddies. I've had enough of that shit."

"I don't know what's best, but I know I've been dreaming about you and I'm dying for you to fuck me again," Tori said, blushing madly.

"I haven't fucked you yet darling," Comanche said with a crooked grin.

"You haven't?"

"No, but I will, if you want me to. I came prepared," she said, standing again and thrusting her hips forward while sticking her fingers in the belt loops of her jeans and pulling them tight.

Tori's eyes got big as she stared at the large bulge where she would expect to see a camel toe. In her imagination she could see the exotic girl between her legs, fucking her silly like her favorite characters in her books did to their girlfriends.

"What ya say, Kitten?"

"Coman...say, what is your name?"

"Linda Smith, believe it or not," she said with an ironic cocking of an eyebrow.

"Smith?"

"My ancestors were civilized," she said, holding up both hands with two fingers to indicate quotes around the word, which came out so full of disdain Tori could feel it.

"I'm sorry," Tori said.

Linda laughed deeply and moved around the desk, pulling Tori to her feet.

"No need for you to be sorry. You didn't do it. I'm long past blaming people, though I'm still an activist for recognition of the wrongs done to us. That doesn't bother you does it?"

"No."

"Good. Now, are you ready for Conan, cause I'm just about to go crazy wanting you," she said seriously.

"I've been wanting you since we left the club," Tori replied after a moment's hesitation.

She didn't know what to expect, but the next thing she knew she was upside down, thrown over the tall girl's shoulder. Tori squealed in surprise and again when Linda tossed her onto the upper bunk. The tall girl climbed up and threw herself on top of Tori with a sexy growl.

Tori felt Linda's hands rip her blouse open, the spray of buttons making hollow sounds as they hit the floor. Linda's mouth was on her neck, sucking so hard it was sure to leave a mark and occasionally nipping. She pulled Tori's bra down beneath her breasts and began to roughly massage them, pinching the nipples and pulling them out from her body.

Tori made a noise that she had never made before. It was part moan, part groan and part whimper. It seemed to set Linda off as she slid down Tori's body and captured a nipple in her mouth. Her teeth were small and sharp and send shivers through Tori's body as the dark headed girl nipped and sucked. Linda's hands found Tori's belt and quickly undid it. In short order, Tori felt her button and the zipper yield to those nimble hands. Linda sat up suddenly, pulling Tori's jeans and panties down her legs.

Tori raised her legs and allowed Linda to pull the jeans off. She lost a shoe in the process and kicked off the other as Linda tossed her jeans to the floor. While still on her knees, Linda opened her fly and pulled out a wicked looking dildo. It was black and fat and drooped under its own weight. Tori felt her insides go all quivery at the sight of it.

Linda fell back onto her then, her mouth again licking and sucking Tori's sensitive nipple while her hand roughly massaged her pussy. Tori groaned when Linda thrust a single finger deeply into her, it was joined almost immediately by a second. Sparks of pleasure shot into her head as those fingers sawed in and out. She arched her back and mewled in pleasure as Linda chewed on her left nipple.

The tall girl sat up abruptly, and caught one of Tori's legs. She heaved it over, forcing the smaller girl to roll over onto her tummy. Linda's hands grabbed her hips and pulled upwards.

"On your knees, bitch," she commanded.

Tori readily complied. Her whole body was quivering with desire and the rough words seemed to twist the knife of desire she felt in her tummy. Linda pushed Tori's legs outwards with her knees and grasped her cock. She rubbed the head up and down Tori's lips.

"Tell me you want it, you hot little bitch."

Tori wanted to speak. She wanted to parrot the words like her fictional heroines did, but she couldn't make her mouth work.

"Tell me you want this big fat toy jammed up into that sweet cunt," Linda demanded.

The sound of Linda's hand smacking her ass was like a shot in the small room. Tori yelped as the hot pain flared and subsided to a penetrating warmth that suffused her cheek.

"See? You can talk. Now tell mummy what you want in that filthy little fuck hole of yours."

The words! They were killing her. Setting her blood on fire and fueling an all consuming need in her pussy. She had no idea how Linda could know, but she didn't care anymore. She just had to get fucked.

"Ohhh, please," Tori groaned.

"Tell me, do you want this nice fat cock?"

"Yes, please" Tori whined.

"Take it!" Linda barked, driving the dildo into Tori with a strong thrust.

She was so wet and ready the toy met little resistance. Tori felt stuffed, and her body jerked as more and more of it was jammed into her. Linda had her hands digging into the flesh of Tori's hips and she was soon pounding into the shuddering girl with abandon.

Tori was in heaven. Her body was responding to the stabbing thrusts, her hips throwing herself back onto the thick toy. Her mind was fogged by a lust she had only dreamed possible. When Linda's hands left her hips and wound into her hair, Tori's breath caught in her throat. The Indian girl pulled back hard, raising Tori to her hands and then bending her back. She used Tori's hair like reins, pulling her back to meet the thrusts as she picked up speed.

The only sounds in the room were the slap of Linda's hips on her ass and the juicy, squishy sounds of the big toy methodically sliding in and out of her sopping pussy.

Tori's body was so tense she felt like every fiber of her being was being stretched to the limit. Tension built in her stomach and lower back until she felt she was about to explode.

"Cum you little slut," Linda gasped.

Tori just fell apart as a massive contraction in her pussy was followed by rapid fire tensing and releasing. Each pulse sent signals to her brain that were so impossibly sharp and pleasurable she had trouble coping. She heard a screeching scream of animal pleasure, but couldn't reconcile that feral sound with anything she could make. Another blast from her pussy sent her reeling off into a place of fantastic shapes and colors and sensations.

She wasn't sure how, but Linda had rolled over on her side. She was holding Tori's leg up and still driving into her pussy. Her free hand had slid to the top of Tori's slit and was grinding on her clitoral area in time to the thrusts. Another orgasm took her with even greater intensity than the first. She was barely coherent when another massive contraction blasted her with pure bliss.

***

The room was warm and dark. Tori had been lying on her back, her head resting on

Linda's arm as she contentedly suckled from one of Linda's big breasts. Linda was smiling and gently stroking her head, brushing stray hairs from her eyes.

"That was incredible," Tori managed at last.

"Better than your books?"

"Definitely."

"Good. I wanted it to be the best for you," Linda said softly.

"I had no idea you were so butch."

Linda laughed softly and gently pulled Tori's head back to her nipple.

"I like it hard sometimes. I like it soft, too. It depends on my mood and my partner's needs. So I can play the top, the big bad butch, or the bottom, it's all good."

"You were just perfect," Tori said dreamily.

"I should think so. I got Jo to show me your stash," she replied, laughing when Tori sat straight up.

"Relax, baby," Linda said, gently pulling her back down to the bed.

Tori was mortified, but Linda held her close and smiled.

"There's nothing wrong with liking it hard. Nothing to be embarrassed about. Everyone has their own little kinks, I'm just glad yours was one I could accommodate."

"It's strange," Tori said finally.

"What's strange?"

"Well. This was perfect, I mean just like I had always imagined it would be. But..."

"But what?"

"But, I really enjoyed it at the club too. I've never had any fantasy like that."

"There's a whole world of variations, kitten. Some you'll like, some you won't, some will be take it or leave it. You never know till you try them. Don't set limits without giving things a try. Just stay honest with me and I'll stay honest with you and we can explore any you wish."

"I'm just..."

"You're just afraid you'll want to try something and I'll think you're a freak," Linda said with a grin.

"Yeah."

"Baby, we're all freaks, every one of us, in our own way. Now I need to go."

"Why?"

"Because you and Jo need to talk and I don't want to get in the way," she said as she climbed out of the bed and stuffed the toy back into her jeans.

"When will I see you again?" Tori asked.

"Tomorrow, if you want to go to dinner with me, I'd love to take you out."

***

Tori was sitting on her bed, when Jo let herself into the room.

"Have fun?" she asked as she took her jacket off.

"She knocked my socks off," Tori replied.

"Good for you," Jo said as she laughed and got a beer out of the fridge.

"Thanks Jo," Tori said quietly.

"If you had told me, you could have been having wild monkey sex all semester."

"I didn't know for sure and it was so embarrassing, ya know?"

"Sure," Jo said.

Tori could feel the discomfort slipping in and she wasn't going to allow it.

"I really didn't know."

"It's cool."

"No, it isn't cool. I hurt you and I'm sorry."

Something in her words made Jo look up and their eyes locked. Jo searched her face and then a smile split her lips.

"It's okay, Tor. You don't have to say anything else. I don't need it. I was hurt, but I really didn't have any right to be, I just assumed there was nothing we couldn't say to each other. I just now realized there were some things you couldn't say to yourself and I should have known that. Friends forever?"

"Forever," Tori said, smiling as she lay back on her bunk.

Student Tribbing with Teacher

Eva has sitting in the front row of the classroom. Mrs Cudna was having one of her last chemistry classes of the year. It was her birthday actually, she was turning 19. She wanted to make herself a great present for her birthday and she had a clear idea about what that best present would be. Eva always had a crush for her teacher. Her libido was tremendous, and Mrs Cudna was always one of her favorite fantasies when masturbating. She used to masturbate daily, and even more than once a day. She always wanted to transform the fantasies with her teacher in reality. She thought that eating her teacher's pussy would be that perfect present for her. She came to school without wearing panties and sitting in the front row she tried several times to simply flash her pussy to Mrs Cudna; she knew that if her teacher was looking at her, she could not miss that. When the class ended and students were preparing to leave the room, Mrs Cudna said,

"Eva, please follow me to my office."

It was a clear evidence to Eva that her flashing was successful and Mrs Cudna noticed it. She was about to get punished for that but she planned to turn that into her advantage and dominate her teacher.

They entered Mrs Cudna office and the teacher had a seat behind her desk, while Eva stood in front.

"What you did today was outrageous," started the teacher. "How did you dare doing that in my class?" She was upset.

"What did I do, Mrs Cudna?" asked Eva innocently.

"You know very well what you did," answered the teacher.

"No ma'am, I don't," insisted the girl.

"Don't insult me pretending that you didn't flash your pussy in my class."

"Oh, that," said Eva, like it all came back to her. "Did you see my pussy?"

"You're damn sure I saw it," said the teacher.

"Did you like it?" asked Eva smiling innocently.

Her questioned left her teacher stoned. She didn't expect that reaction and question from Eva.

"I... I..." she was speechless in front of the girl.

"If you're not sure I can show it to you again," said Eva.

Saying that she grabbed her skirt and without giving the opportunity to her teacher to say anything she raised the skirt, exposing her hairless beautiful young pussy to her teacher. Mrs Cudna was literally left with her mouth opened. Out of the sudden she was in a defensive position in front of the girl.

"I hope you do like it Mrs Cudna," said Eva. After a pause she added. "I think it's a lovely pussy."

She smiled again and she realized she was able to take the control of the entire discussion. From that point it was only up to her what to do with Mrs Cudna.

"Do you have a beautiful pussy yourself, Mrs Cudna?" asked Eva.

The teacher shocked this time. She didn't know what to do, but the boldness of the girl opened her mouth and answer.

"I don't know," she said, and she realized her chances to punish Eva vanished and she was no longer in control of the situation.

"Then you better show me," said Eva. "Because I can definitely tell."

Mrs Cudna did listen to her and after moments of silence she finally said,

"You want me to show you my pussy?"

"Of course," she answered. "I wanted to see your pussy for a long time. I shown you mine, now it's time you show me yours."

"But..." started the teacher.

"No buts, Mrs Cudna," interrupted Eva. "Take off your cloths and show me your pussy. Now!" she said and made it sound like an order.

Mrs Cudna stood there for a few moments, then a powerful force drove her to follow Eva's order. She was under the spell of the bold girl. She stood up and removed her skirt and panties, exposing her pussy, covered with a nicely trimmed bush.

"Sit down," demanded Eva. "And open your legs."

Mrs Cudna executed and Eva came to her and sat between her legs. She admired the teacher's pussy and said,

"Beautiful. It's my favorite kind of pussy. Plum, with big fat lips, nicely trimmed."

Saying that she put her right hand on teacher's pussy and caressed it.

"I masturbate every day fantasizing about you. Now I finally have the chance to eat your pussy."

Saying that she dived between her teacher's legs and kissed her fat pussy. She started to lick it, up and down, and sucked on the clitoris. The teacher was in a state between resiting and pleasure. But the girl was in complete control of her.

"This is one of the best pussy I ever ate," said Eva. "And I ate a lot," she added. "You taste great."

"Thank you," said Mrs Cudna and was actually surprised to hear herself saying that.

Eva put a finger inside her pussy and get the moisture from it. She then raised it to her teacher's mouth and said,

"Taste it!"

She put it in her mouth and Mrs Cudna tasted her pussy juices for the first time in her life.

"I hope you like it because it's fantastic."

She continued to eat on her teacher's pussy for a while. Mrs Cudna lost any resistance and left herself into Eva's game. The pleasure was building gradually in her body. The girl was such a great pussy eater. She never had her pussy eaten that way in her entire life. She started to moan and shiver, especially when Eva was sucking or pushing her tongue against her swollen clit. After minutes of eating, Mrs Cudna exploded into a powerful orgasm, moaning extremely load and trembling from her entire body. It was the most powerful orgasm she remembered in a long time. Eva licked her clean for a while, until the teacher relaxed in her chair and in Eva's arms.

After finishing her teacher Eva stood up and looked at the desk behind her. With a single moved she swiped it, throwing everything from it on the floor.

"Why did you do that?" the teacher dared to ask.

"My greatest fantasy is tribbing you. Take off the rest of your cloths and get on the table."

"Tribbing me?" asked the teacher. "What is that?"

"That is crossing our legs and rubbing our pussies against each other until we cum," explained Eva.

Saying that she began to undress and remained naked, exposing her beautiful young body, her firm, tanned, big tits, her great ass and legs, her bald pussy, everything. She looked at her teacher expecting her to undress; Mrs Cudna, seeing the girl standing there for her to execute did as she was told and took off her shirt and bra, releasing her large, soft, milky tits, and standing completely naked in front of the girl. She felt a little bit humiliated, being reduced to a simple toy, but the thought of another orgasm like the one she just experience drove her to do exactly as told.

"Get on the table," said Eva again, and the teacher followed the request and sat on her office desk, on her back.

Eva climbed after her and spread Mrs Cudna's legs and leaned over her, their bodies touching and their pussies pressing on each other. She started moving slowly up and down so that their pussies, and especially their clits would rub on each other. She then simulated fucking just like she was a man, except that she was using her pussy to press onto her teacher's pussy. After a while she changed her position, crossing her legs with the teacher thus being able to touch their pussies much better. She held Mrs Cudna's left foot in the air, and she started to move her body just like she was riding. She gradually increased her movements and the effort made first her, and then the teacher moan. Their pussies were rubbing faster and faster, harder and harder with each moment, taking more effort from both of them and making them moan and breath heavily. To her own surprise, Mrs Cudna enjoyed it very much and was putting all her efforts into the tribbing. She wanted to cum again, and she wanted to cum onto Eva's pussy. The girl was riding her like crazy and eventually they both cum. It was the teacher that cum first, for the second time in ten minutes, and only a few seconds later, Eva exploded in a powerful orgasm. Cuming together with her teacher was her long time dream, and it proved such a great experience that ended with such a powerful orgasm.

She collapsed into Mrs Cudna arms and they spent the next couple of minutes restoring their breaths. It was the teacher that eventually broke the silence saying,

"Oh, this was wonderful. Something that I never imaged I would do."

"Yes, Mrs Cudna. I never enjoyed fucking someone so much. You are so wonderful." She said all that while resting her head on her teacher's large chest.

"I hope we can do this again," the teacher said.

"Yes, once you did it, it's catching. But you can be sure we will do this again," said Eva.

"I hope I will be excused for flashing my pussy in your classroom," said Eva smiling, while standing up.

"Of course child. You are excused," said Mrs Cudna.

"Then I should catch the bus home," said Eva.

They dressed in silence and Eva left her teacher's office, but not before giving her a kiss. The teacher remained in the office for the next half an hour meditating to her amazing experience with her student. The girl was unbelievable.

Sue Shows Off to Vera

I was 28 years old and a divorcee. Over the years I had had some form of sex or another with about ten men and two women. The first of the lesbian encounters had been my college roommate my first encounter with my second partner had included my partner's husband. Later we met often and alone.

My name is Sue. This tale is about my third encounter with a female. I am taller than most women at 5'8". I am a bit athletic so my body is somewhat firm without being muscled up. My bra when I wear one has a B cup but mostly I don't wear one.

They say that being into either sex doubles your chance for a Saturday night date. It seems to me that the same things that constitute flirting with men also seem to work with women. So I do flirt with women often and occasionally I encounter someone I want. Such was my experience with Vera.

A new couple had moved into the adjacent unit which was a mirror image to mine. She was Vera he was Ed. Each unit was L shaped with the master bedroom at the end and a small court in between. I watched them move in and flirted briefly with them both. Happily I was sensing interest from both.

Vera appeared to be about my age. She had short dark hair and a well shaped body. She was about three inches shorter than me.

Later as I went to close my bedroom window a naughty thought made it's way into my brain. The building being build on a hill their apartment was several feet above mine. "I'll bet that they can see right into my room." I thought. My devious brain began looking around my bedroom considering various plans.

Soon I was hard at work relocating my furniture. I gave them a direct side view of the bed and a reflected view of most of the rest of the room off my various mirrors should they look out of their window.

I had never considered myself an exhibitionist but somehow the idea of becoming one was exciting to me. As testament to that fact my panty crotch was soaked as I completed my preparations.

That evening I pulled back the covers on my bed then put a bright red dildo, a gift with it's own story, on the lower sheet right in plain sight. I turned on the bedside lamp and adjusted the light to spotlight the dildo.

My hope was that in spite of the distance that they would identify the dildo. It was a very dark night. I left the bedroom light on then slipped out onto the dark balcony. I positioned myself so as to be able to see if either looked out their window.

Sure enough about a half hour later I caught the glint of light off of glass and the outline of a body in their window. Then I knew that my instincts had been right, someone was looking into my room with field glasses. With that, I reentered my bedroom, got naked and entered the lighted area. Then I picked up my dildo and turned off the light.

The exhibitionist in me was awakened. By the time just a minute or two later that the head of Little Red met my cunt opening I was so wet and slippery that it was able to enter me easily. As I fucked myself I thought about leaving the light on next time. The thought of being watched as I masturbated brought me to a quick extra special orgasm.

When I was done I turned on the light as I got out of bed. I parked Red in the drawer of my night stand. I then stood and walked to the bathroom. Still naked of course. I hoped that someone was watching but I sincerely doubted it.

Next morning on my way to my car I found myself parked next to Vera. As we approached our cars I noticed that Vera was wearing a knee length skirt with a thin knitted top. Her breasts were a nice size and they seemed to make little tents in the top where her nipples might be as she spotted me.

"Hi Sue. Sleep well?" She asked with a little wink.

"Finally," I replied. "I had to use a sleep aid." With that I winked back at her. The exchange made my pussy tingle. After a minute I said.

"If you guys are sufficiently moved in how about coming over for a drink after dinner."

"Love to." Replied Vera. "About eight OK?"

"Just right. I'll be expecting you."

They were prompt and brought me a small bunch of field flowers. The visit was enjoyable. It soon became obvious that although Vera and Ed were still very much sexually involved they were not immune to outside interests.

We got together often. We all teased each other and I continued putting my shows occasionally but what I had first hoped might turn into a roaring threesome did not happen. Nor did anything happen between Vera and I until several months later.

Vera meanwhile had become my best friend. There had been a lot of flirting between us but no overt contact. One evening she and I attended our first ever Erotic Women's Products party at the home of my friend Ann. It was a fun time as those of you who have attended such a party can attest to.

It was also a horny time for most as many toys and lotions were passed around. Some were tried while other's were discussed in detail. As the party progressed you could smell the female sexual arousal in the room. The women's voices became more husky and the eyes became somewhat glazed and breathing seemed to become more labored.

I was certainly no exception. By the time the party was over I was very wet and downright horny. As per our plan Vera was spending the night with me. As the party had progressed I became increasingly hopeful about the evening's outcome.

Her husband was out of town. When we arrived home Vera still seemed excited and I assumed horny as we discussed what we had seen and experienced at the party.

We had a drink to settle us down as we undressed, did our bathroom chores and went to bed. Vera was obviously naked under her shorty nightgown. She had nice tits which she seem to flash regularly and the sight of which almost always caused a twinge between my legs. I too was in a shorty nightgown.

The drink had done nothing to settle me down. As if echoing my thoughts Vera said.

"I thought the drink would settle me down but if anything I'm even more horny now. Must be the company."

I didn't answer, I didn't dare, I might give myself away. It was a warm night so we needed little in the line of bed covering. After some scrunching around we ended covered only by a sheet pulled up over our waists. Suddenly Vera said.

"That meeting really did a job on me. If Ed were here I'd be tearing his cloths off and riding his cock like a Rodeo rider." After another minute she added.

"Would you mind very much if I solved my problem? I'd really love it if you could join me. That would really make my visit complete."

"I've been doing without for quite awhile so I won't promise to be on my best behavior. I have big hopes for the three toys I ordered to replace my nearly worn out dildos. But until then I'm dangerous to be around.

"There's just you and me." She said. "I won't tell if you don't."

As she spoke I saw Vera's hand move down and begin to tug her nightie up. She quickly began to massage the inside of her upper thigh. A minute or two went by before she asked. "I always been curious. Have you ever done 'IT'?"

She didn't define 'IT' but there was no doubt in my mind what she meant. The twinges in my pussy increased in intensity as I considered my reply.

"By it I assume that you are speaking of the lesbian stuff?" Vera nodded. "In that case I admit that I've been known to practice that particular depravity........... With much enjoyment I might add."

I didn't say anything for another moment then I added. "Now that the subject has been brought up. How about you?"

"Oh I've thought about it, I've often diddled myself fantasizing about it but obviously I've never done anything about it except for some kissing once. That was interrupted before it got very far. I've always been afraid to mention it. But tonight I'm so horny that I got brave and brought it up."

"Do you mean to say that I've been the subject of your fantasy?" I asked.

Vera hesitated a while before saying. "Vera honey I have wanted to do things with other girls since I understood that girls often did things with other girls. Since we've met your face has been my visual during many an orgasm."

Her remark went from my ears straight down to my pussy. My favorite recent lesbian fantasy was fucking Vera with a dildo as I licked her clit. My mouth got ahead of my brain and asked.

"Vera, have you ever tried a dildo?"

"Not a real one but I have tried various other things and find them very effective. How about you?"

I hesitated. "I have two. Would you like to try one?"

I reached over and opened the drawer of the bedside table next to me. "Handy, don't you think?"

I opened the drawer and brought out both. Both were round and shaped with various bulges and wide places. They had been painted with many coats of red paint and were very shiny. One was considerably larger round and longer than the other.

At the same time I had a mental image of Vera making love to herself with the big one. It was a very exciting thought.

"You want me to try one?" Vera asked, her voice choked. "God, I'm so horny. Yes! It's been a long time since I've felt so excited.....Yes."

"Which one do you want?" I asked.

"I'd love to try the big one. I've never had anything so big inside of me. I'm so wet and ready I think I'm ready for something like that. I ordered a big vibrator tonight."

"I can't always handle the big one," I said. "I have to really be hot and slippery to handle it, but when I do, God, I love it."

As I handed Vera the bigger one I said. "Meet 'Big Red' I've named them, 'Little Red' and 'Big Red'."

"Little Red, do your duty." I said as I plunged Little Red into my hot vagina I wanted to start before Vera could change her mind.

"Wow, that feels good tonight." I said as I began to plunge it in and out of my slippery cunt, fucking myself.

Vera meanwhile had set Big Red beside her and was energetically plunging two fingers in and out of herself with one hand while fingering her clit with the other. It was only seconds later when I heard her gentle moans which were much like the sounds I make as I approach orgasm.

I repositioned myself so that I could watch her face. Her head was thrown back, her eyes were closed, her lips were parted, her whole face showed her to clearly be in the midst of a very pleasurable experience. She was beautiful.

The sight propelled me toward my own orgasm. My wrist seemed to develop a mind of it's own. I was holding Red with three fingers at it's very outer end. It was almost disappearing inside of me as I raced to make it bring me to completion. Suddenly my pelvis began to jump up and down off the bed just as it does when a real cock is bringing me to completion.

I was making those same sounds Vera was making as she orgasamed then without conscious thought I heard myself saying.

"Vera, Vera, let me show you how. Let me fuck you with 'Big Red'. I want him to fuck you as I lick your clit, I've wanted to do that for such a long time now. Please darling let me pleasure you. Please, please."

Then I realized that Vera's face was now only inches away from mine, that her lips were approaching. Just a couple of seconds later we were kissing, kissing gently, kissing erotically. My tongue was sweeping back and forth across her slightly parted lips just the way I was so anxious to do to those other lips, only a short distance below.

Then I felt my hand being removed from 'Little Red' and something replaced him. I instantly recognized that Big Red was being handed to me. Vera then reached further and found 'Little Red', a brief moment later Little Red began fucking me again.

We continued to kiss, mouths open. Our tongues became very busy doing incredible things to each other's bodies. I guided the head of Big Red to Vera's crotch. It found the swollen lips of her labia and slipped it between them. I teased Vera with Red for a minute sliding it up and down her vulva until she whimpered into my mouth.

"Now Sue darling, now, stick him into me now! Fuck me with him. I've waited so long for a moment like this. Now, please."

I was afraid to plunge him into her quickly as I had plunged his little brother into my cunt. I found her opening and began to work it open with the head of Big Red. I had slowly and gently pushed him about two inches into Vera when she humped herself up against my hand causing him to slide well up inside of her cunt.

Her cunt apparently was so wet and slippery with desire that it was an easy trip. I heard her gasp with pleasure at the act.

I held Big Red steady as I broke our mouth to mouth kiss bending to kiss my way down Vera's body stopping at her breasts to give her protruding nipples some extra attention. Soon I arrived at my target. Seconds later for the first time I began to tongue Vera's clit. Immediately my tongue sought and found that mini penis that is the center of the female sexual excitment.

Vera's body leaped against my mouth at my tongue's touch. Meanwhile I was suffering my own mini convulsions as Vera pumped Little Red in and out of my slippery pussy. I loved it being done to me even more than doing it to myself. It was about the size of most cocks of my experience but never had I felt a cock so hard and unyielding.

The fact that it was Vera doing it to me invoked in me a passion level that I had seldom felt. I was well on my way to my orgasm enjoying what was being done to me and at the same time concentrating on my efforts to bring erotic joy to Vera.

At that moment I felt movements begin against my tongue that signaled that my newest lover was about to orgasm. I was very happy with myself feeling an immense joy for causing it to happen.. I was also happy that our orgasms would be almost simultaneous.

Vera's fist was slamming rapidly against my body as she pounded the dildo in and out of my aching cunt. My body was responding in time with her hand movements. I could hear Vera almost begging as she was saying.

"Sue, Sue darling, come for me, come with me, I'm about to come, it feels so good, let's do this forever, come now, please."

By then both our bodies were quaking and trembling and shaking. Never had I felt a woman come so joyously before. The excitment my body felt as it duplicated what I was feeling happen in Vera's body was unlike anything else in my experience .

Moments later we were both exhausted. I fell back on the bed, my legs spread, the dildo, now stationary sticking out of me. I let go of Big Red as Vera assumed a similar position. Gradually I came alive and began to feel my body begin to stir.

I laid my head on Vera's thigh and reached for Big Red. I slowly and gently pulled it out of her until it released accompanied by a plopping sound. I began to kiss her thigh as I reached my other arm around and under her other thigh until I reached her pussy with my fingers.

I used them to spread her labia as I kissed and licked my way toward it her pussy. When I reached it I used my tongue to examined one side all the way up one side and down the other side. I took several trips each way before I made my first stop at her clit.

I examined her clitoral area thoroughly with my tongue then proceeded downward to her vaginal opening. My tongue then examined it completely probing here and there and then penetrating it as deep as I could with my busy tongue.

Vera was obviously enjoying my efforts. She came with a full body orgasm that had her shaking and twisting and moaning. She was not quite over it when her mouth somehow sucked my whole clitoral area into her mouth and her lively tongue played a tune on my clit.

Meanwhile she again began fucking me with Little Red quickly bringing me to one of the best orgasms I could remember.

Needless to say that by the time the visit was over we both had to admit that we had each been thoroughly satisfied by the other.

Surprise in a Taxi

Fearing that I might become a target for unwelcome attentions, I tried to hail a cab but as is ususal, you can never get one when it's raining! But against all the odds, that symbol of trustworthiness, a black London taxicab, pulled up right alongside where I was standing. The back door swung open and without even speaking to the driver I jumped in and slammed the door.

As soon as I realised the cab was already occupied I apologised profusely and reached to open the door, but the woman sitting in the back seat stopped me and asked where I was headed. Nervously I told her roughly where I lived and she assured me that was close to her destination and that I was welcome to share her cab. Looking out at the torrential rainstorm, I accepted her offer willingly.

The skies were dark and the windows were steamed up with condensation so we could not see out, and no-one could see in either. The driver took no notice of us as he weaved his way through the dense city-centre traffic. My dark-haired olive-skinned companion made polite small talk, speaking in a husky voice with a mysterious hint of South American accent. She became more animated and demonstrative, touching my arm, then my leg. The sky outside was black as night and I found it difficult to see her face in the gloom. The air in the taxi has hot and humid and my rain-soaked dress and hair clung wetly to my skin. The atmosphere was highly charged but I froze with complete shock when my car-share partner slid one hand up my thigh and under the hem of my clingy dress.

I stayed motionless, unsure how to react and, perhaps assuming I had given my tacit approval, she placed her other hand over my breast, squeezing it as she slid her left hand further up my leg. My mind raced as she moved her hand up my inner thigh then cupped it over my mound. My pants were damp, but not from the rain, and offered little protection from her probing fingers. She placed her middle finger directly over my slit and pressed through the thin white material. I felt my soft flesh yield to her touch and my outer lips parted. Without a word she then hooked a finger inside the small triangle of my pants and described small circles over the meticulously-shaven skin of my outer labial lips.

"You're so smooth, darling" she purred.

I lay back and parted my legs, sending to her the clearest signal that I approved of what she was doing and that I did not want her to stop. I didn't care any more about the driver, or the rain, or getting home. I was so excited by the shear audacity and presumptiveness of my fellow traveller.

She did not look at me but continued to look straight ahead, or out of the window. I tried to keep quiet but I couldn't stop myself from moaning under my breath and whispering words of encouragement. Whenever a particularly noisy vehicle passed us, I cried out louder to release my tension and to accentuate the pleasure. Now she had her whole hand inside my thong pants, pulling them away from the blossoming petals of my gaping pussy and forcing the narrow strip of material at the back deep into my bum crack where it teased my anus.

My mystery guest slid several of her fingers inside my vagina and positioned her thumb on my clit, rubbing me from side to side and up and down. Periodically, she withdrew her fingers from my opening and slid them upwards, depositing more of my copious lube onto my swollen, twitching clit. Then she returned her thumb to my slippery bud; each time I nearly screamed as she slid it ever-so-lightly over my wet, aching clitoris.

I spread my legs as wide as they would go and lifted my bum off the seat. The hem of my dress was up around my waist and the leather seat of the taxi was cold and sticky against the backs of my thighs. I closed my eyes and tilted back my head, concentrating hard on my surprise companion's expert movements. Just at that moment, the taxi rumbled over some cobblestones and the vibration tipped me over the edge. She removed her hand from my breast and placed it over my mouth to muffle my yell as she milked a long and powerful climax from the inner folds of my cunt.

As soon as the taxi stopped at the next set of lights, she jumped out spoke to the driver, stuffing a large-denomination note into his hand. She motioned towards me and he turned around, just as I had pulled down my dress and was combing my tousled hair coarsely back into place.

"Where to, miss?" he asked.

I cleared my parched, dry throat and barely managed to croak my address. I looked out of the side window and she had already disappeared into the crowd.

The taxi pulled up outside my apartment and I stumbled out into the rain. As I closed my front door I pondered on the experience. Maybe she knew me and we would meet again? Or maybe it is better that we don't and I can relive the experience in my memory.

Swim Coach and Friend Seduce Coed

I'm a college swim coach, 39, with short black hair, 5'4" 120 lbs. After our great winning season I had a party and invited all the girls on the swim team After the party my girlfriend Katie, who is 36, blonde and in very good shape, said that she would help me clean up. I said don't take it all on yourself; ask one of the girls to help.

Well,she said, "there's this cute girl who keeps gazing at me who would make a great volunteer"

"You are soooo bad," I replied, "as long as we get this mess cleaned up before next week I don't care who helps."

Most of our guest were exiting when I noticed that Mandy and Katie were doing more gabbing than cleaning up. So I went outside and told them I had this great bottle of wine we could open if this all gets cleaned up by nightfall.

As I got closer, I noticed what Katie was noticing, which was that Mandy was very beautiful, with long dark hair and piercing blue eyes. Our eyes met and her smile melted me.

"That would be great Ms. Smythe, and afterward, maybe we could take a dip in your hot tub!"

I couldn't wait to see her out of her skirt and top. She had very generous chest with very pert nipples. Her 19 year old body was so tight and firm. I had never noticed her at practice and assumed she was one of new freshman girls or a tranfer student. After cleaning up in the kitchen I came out to find Katie and Mandy already changing.

I joined them and we all hopped into the hot tub in our bikinis.

We proceeded to converse about the season when I noticed that Mandy seemed a little distracted. It was then that I noticed that Katie had her foot between Mandy's thighs. As we chatted she had surreptitiously slid her foot there and Mandy was letting her tease her thru her bikini bottoms. I pretended not to notice from this point to see how far this would go. After a while Katie invited her to sit closer because "this jet here feels so good against my lower back, here...try it..."

When the bubbles parted slightly I could see that Katie had slipped down Mandy's bottoms and was very delicately exploring our young friend's vaginal petals with her fingers, making sure, or so she thought, that I didn't notice.

"Well," I finally announced, "this is my house and if anyone is going to have any fun, I want to play too..."

They both looked stunned.

With that I slid over and reached down to find my girlfriend's hand fully feeling Mandy's sweet mound.

"I see....you sure this is ok mandy? Katie's not pressuring you is she?"

Mandy nodded no, saying "I've never been with a girl before, but I've often fantasized about it. I guess if I'm enjoying this I should at least not stop what feels so natural. Are the two of you lovers?"

"Yes," said Katie, "we've lived together for about a year and we both find you absolutely adorable."

With that I tugged down her bottoms completely and proceeded to move into kiss her.

She parted her lips slightly and I darted my tongue between them. She accepted my tongue lovingly and darted her own out to explore my very willing mouth.

Katie wanted a turn kissing this pretty young girl. Katie's lips moved to Mandy's open lips and Mandy let her kiss her very deeply also. I loved watching my lover enjoy this sweet young coed. Their lips were now locked and instead of jealousy all I could feel was excitement and anticipation of what I would do to her next. I reached behind her to undo her top...she stopped me and suggested we should get more privacy.

I agreed and we grabbed some towels and proceeding upstairs to my master bedroom. I peaked between her legs and noticed her trimmed pussy hair exposed very pouty lips.

I locked the door and we arranged ourselves with her in the middle of the bed.

I removed my top and bottoms and Katie did the same. Our nude moist bodies were cooled by the air outside the tub and all our nipples were quite hard.

Katie then said to Mandy, "you have to most gorgeous breasts i've seen on a girl your age."

Mandy replied, "will you two promise me that this will be our secret, I have a fiance who's in politics and if it got out that I was bi it would be scandalous"

"No problem" we said, "as long as you let us suckle those perfect breasts. She nodded vigorously, as we descended on her gorgeous body.

I took the left one and Katie the right. Mandy's moans filled the room as our tongues ran circles around her pouty aerolas. We teased them then each began suckling them hungrily. Mandy loved it hold us tightly against her and beginning to moan louder and louder.

After a few succulent minutes we slid down her body and spread her firm thighs wide apart. Our fingers spreading her now moistened petals. Her pink inner folds now explosed to our curious tongues.

We could barely stop ourselves as we each took turns nibbling her clitty until it was visibly throbbing. Finally, she begged us to let her cum. I dove in and slid my tongue deep inside her cunny, exploring her pink center. I wiggled my tongue in deep, devouring her now flooding juices. Then I moved out and took her clitty between my lips and tongue lashed it. I watched as Katie held her as her body began convulsing with delight. As she came she screamed for more. Katie could take no more and moved up to straddle her adorable face, slowly sliding her own pussy to her for her enjoyment. Mandy closed her legs when she could take no more. I moved next to them to pinch Katie's nipples as she rode our adorable new friend.

Katie's pussy pressed down tight as Mandy pushed her tongue inside.

Then with a gentle moan, Katie trembled letting a sweet stream of juices into Mandy's hungry mouth, cumming as hard as I've ever seen her cum.

Katie collapsed on top of us and we all giggled and held each other tight, all falling into a deep sleep.

T'N'A (Tongue In Ass)

Dana kneeled on the bed with her face resting on the feather pillow, her blue tee-shirt sliding down her flawless back. She slid the ice cube up and down her ass crack, her body heat melting it and letting it drip down to her hairless puss and letting it run down her smooth thighs. Her hands were slippery with the water. She pushed the shrinking ice cube into her asshole and used her well used anal muscles to expel it smoothly back into her hand. She had given herself an enema earlier so she was very clean. She cupped the ice cube in her palm and rubbed it up and down her glistening, pink slit. The heat from her pussy melting the ice cube even more. She pushed the cold phallus into her hot puss and her breath caught in her lungs from the sweet sensations. Dana then pushed two well manicured fingers into her hot/cold puss and began fingering slowly while pushing the ice cube deeper inside of her until it bottomed out at her cervix. She brought her wet fingers to her lips and tasted the water and her sticky juices. The cold inside made her convulse several times.

She reached over into the ice bucket beside the bed for the umpteenth time that morning for yet another cube. This time she rolled the ice cube back and forth over her taut anus. Her other hand was busy revolving the fingers around and around her pouting clitoris. She delayed her orgasm as long as she could. She enjoyed coming to the brink only to wash away and come again a short while later. A few cubes later she was biting the pillow as one hand stuffed the melting ice into her ass with two long fingers, while the other hand rubbed the water running down her slit into the pink pearl that was her clit.

Dana's knees slid out from under her and she basked in the glow of her hour's worth of masturbation. Her fingers slid out of her pink ass and found their way into her mouth where she sucked the water from them. The ice cube meanwhile was numbing her bowels in a pleasant sort of way. Dana's gooey cum leaked out from between her puffy, hairless pussy lips to puddle on the sheets. She had a few after shocks of orgasm, and she shook with them and smiled.

Soon she sat up and tossed her short, blond hair out of her face. She got up and looked out the window her blue shirt falling back down to cover half of her petite body. The other half remained naked, and she enjoyed the exhibitionism were any passerby to glance up at her apartment window. She stretched her arms above her and her breasts rose with the movement.

She turned and saw her gooey cum soaking into the sheets. Smiling she took the two steps towards the bed and climbed back onto it on all fours. She dipped her head low like an animal and licked her own cum from the fabric of her bed. It took a few passes with her pink little tongue to get it all, but it was worth it. She then hopped off the bed and walked to the kitchen.

Her thighs were dripping with her watered down juices. She casually ran her hand up one thigh, collecting the wetness on her hand and brought it to her mouth to be eaten. She did the same with her other thigh. Then she brought her hand between her legs and ran her fingers between her hairless pussy, coating them with the remainder of her orgasm and also brought the digits to her mouth to be cleaned.

"Good to the last drop!" she said out loud to the empty apartment.

In the kitchen she went to the fridge and got out a raspberry wine cooler to wash down her 'pre-breakfast'. She brought the beverage back into the bedroom where she pondered what to wear, or what not to wear. It was a struggle as she tried on several outfits, but one in which she prevailed. She emerged from the bedroom in a short, red mini-skirt, sans panties, and a tight, white tank top that pressed her delicious small tits against her chest, sans bra. She was ready to take on the world. Whether or not the world was ready for her was another matter altogether.

At the counter near the door to leave she grabbed her pink purse and paused long enough to slide her small feet into a pair of sandals.

Outside the summer sun felt wonderful. She reached into her purse and pulled out a pair of sunglasses to ease her eyes. She walked with a hungry tummy to the nearest café a few blocks away. She passed the summer parade of flesh as she walked. It was hot out and people wore next to nothing in terms of clothes. Her eyes caught a guy staring at her as he walked near. When he passed he greeted her with a warm hello and she politely did the same.

On the other hand when a scrumptious brunette walked past she was the one with the smiling hello, which was mirrored back to her in the brunette's beautiful face. Dana didn't mind guys that much. Every once in a great, great, great, great, great, great while it was nice to have sex with them, if only to remind her why she preferred women.

She reached the café and went inside. She paused during the transition from the brightness outside to the softer light inside. She took off her glasses and placed them in her purse and walked up to the counter to wait her turn in the short line of customers. She ordered a bagel with cream cheese, a blueberry muffin, and an iced tea. As she sat at an empty table near the window she silently wished her drink was a long island iced tea. She ate in silence watching the people outside walking, switching to watching the other patrons of the café.

She noticed a beautiful Latin lady watching her from a few tables over. Dana smiled at her and the Latina smiled back. Feeling a bit naughty, Dana 'accidentally' knocked her purse to the floor spilling some of its contents. Dana made a face then got out of her seat and squatted to pick the items up. She was careful to give the Latina a wonderful view up her red skirt. When she was done she sat back down and flashed the Latina a wicked smile whom she knew watched the entire voyeuristic episode.

She was looking out the window again at a gorgeous blonde walking in a tight pair of biking shorts that outlined her pussy deliciously when she was startled by a hand placed gently on her shoulder.

"I'm sorry, did I scare you?" The Latina asked. She was beautiful, with soft features, a full chest and nice hourglass hips tapering down into strong thighs. She was wearing tan shorts and a tee shirt, and had an 'I'll fuck you' smile on.

"A little," Dana said and fidgeted in her seat. It was all part of the game you see, to act all innocent and shy when seducing a potential lover. "Please, sit." She gestured to the empty chair across from her.

"Thank you," the Latina smiled and sat down, placing her own drink on the table before her.

"My name is Dana."

"I'm Ada." The beautiful Latina said. Boldly she explained her reason for coming over. "I couldn't help but notice your dilemma earlier."

"When I spilled my purse? Yeah, it was a little embarrassing." Dana said shyly and took a drink of her iced tea.

"Quite." Ada said, "But that's not what I meant." Puzzled Dana asked what she meant. "I meant the fact that you were flashing me." Ada said with a coy smile.

"Was I? I'm sorry, I didn't realize." Dana said biting her lower lip in an act of vulnerable invitation and Ada took the opportunity offered.

"It's alright, think nothing of it. If it wasn't for the innocent flash I might not have had the nerve to come and talk to you with a conversation ice breaker."

Dana thought of that morning and the plentiful bucket of ice next to her bed and she shivered with the memory.

"Are you cold?" Ada asked noticing the shiver.

"A little," Dana shrugged her shoulders with indifference.

"I can see why." Ada said with a mischievous smile on her face as she took a drink from her glass.

"What're you drinking?" Dana asked.

"It's not fuzzy navel I can assure you." Ada said.

Dana was reminded again of her earlier thought about how she wished she had a long island iced tea. She smiled deep and warm at the beautiful woman across from her.

"I tell you what," Ada began, "This is very forward of me, but if you're not busy would you like to come back to my place?" Ada leaned forward for emphasis resting her marvelous breasts on her forearms.

Dana paused for dramatic effect; she was no amateur at this game. Her face was expressionless for a moment before brightening with an inviting smile. "I'd love to."

"Shall we?" Ada asked. Dana nodded in consent.

They both got up and left the soft light of the café. Donning their sunglasses they went out into the blinding brightness of the day's sun. Ada led Dana to her Lexus and they both got in. The windows were soon rolled down and they were driving away.

"Did you have your own car?" Ada asked.

"No, I walked. I only live two blocks from the café." She said looking Ada's body over from behind the confines of her sunglasses.

"Say sweetheart," Ada said disarmingly, "Why don't you give me a peek of that pretty little thing you flashed me back at the café." Dana looked at Ada, and Ada looked right back at her with a smile. Dana smiled as she lifted her red mini-skirt. She also scooted down in the seat further so she could tilt her hips, and with her legs slightly spread offer Ada a pleasant view of her sex.

"How's that?" Dana asked.

Ada reached over with one hand and slid her finger up and down Dana's wet slit. "It's a start," Ada said and smiled again. She took her finger away from Dana's pussy and brought it to her nose and inhaled her scent like a wine connoisseur smelling for a bouquet. Then she placed the finger in her mouth and sucked the wetness from it like a child and the frosting from a cake.

"You smell and taste divine." Ada complimented.

"Thank you," Dana said as her own hand found her slit and was lazily tracing the contours of skin. "I can't wait to return the favor."

"You're going to have to." Ada said then laughed.

"I suppose I will at that." Dana said and laughed with her.

"Don't worry sweetheart, it won't be for much longer," Ada said comfortingly.

Dana hummed in approval, "Good."

Soon they arrived at Ada's condominium and were shortly inside the lush apartment. Dana followed Ada's lovely shaped buttocks into the kitchen where she placed her purse and gestured for Dana to do the same.

"What would you like to drink? I've been on this flavored vodka kick, but it fucks me up too much!" Ada laughed.

"Sounds like fun!" Dana said approvingly, "Pour me some."

Ada got two glasses out of the cupboard and poured each drink. With her drink in hand she walked over to Dana who had wandered towards the terrace. She offered Dana the glass and she took it and sipped gingerly at it.

"We really don't need this to loosen us up, do we sweetheart?" Ada said referring to their drinks.

"No, I don't believe so." Dana said.

"So what would you like to do?" Ada asked sliding up next to Dana so that they were touching.

With a serious tone in her voice Dana broke her façade of innocence. "I want you to do to me anything you want to." Dana took another calming drink.

"Anything?"

"Anything."

Ada took both of their glasses optimistically half-full and placed them on a nearby table. She then took hold of Dana's hand in hers and led her to the bedroom. Ada gestured for Dana to sit on the bed and Dana melted into the down filled comforter. Ada knelt on the floor before her and helped Dana push the red mini-skirt up around her waist. Dana lay back on the down comforter and lost herself in Ada's mouth as she worked her tongue inside her pussy. Ada touched all of those most sensitive places that women know how to touch. She ate up every delicious bit of Dana's pussy. And when Dana came Ada lapped it out of her pussy like a dog, drinking down the sticky juices deep into her belly.

"That was wonderful," Dana said with eyes closed as Ada crept up from her position between Dana's legs.

"That was a beginning," Ada replied. She came back shortly with a latex glove on her right hand.

"Anything?" Ada asked of Dana again.

Dana's smile went from ear to ear. "Anything,"
"Pull your knees to your tits then." Dana did as she was told, leaving herself open, vulnerable, and waiting with a burning anticipation for what was to come.

Ada's wonderful tongue started its journey at her clit where it went in several sweet circles. It wandered down Dana's wet slit where it stroked the pink flesh up and down several times teasing and tasting. It slid across her perenium then ran across her asshole and stabbed itself into the yielding flesh repeatedly.

Dana loved having her ass licked. She liked it even more when she was giving. She liked it the best though when in a sixty-nine and both could devour that most taboo of erotic areas.

Ada licked and kissed on Dana's sweet, sweet asshole. She sucked on it and stabbed it with her tongue going as deep into Dana's bowels as she could possibly manage. She leaned back and spit at Dana's hole and spread it around her ass with her mouth. Dana held her knees to her chest with trembling hands as Ada worked her tongue inside and out of her ass. Ada's nose was digging into Dana's pussy as she worked her tongue in her ass, and Dana loved every second of it.

Then Ada's mouth and tongue and nose were gone. Just as Dana was opening her eyes to see what was happening Ada gently pressed a gloved finger at her anus. Dana's eyes went wide with surprise then relaxed with the comfortable feeling of fingers in her butt.

"You like it?" Ada asked slightly surprised herself.

"I love it!" Dana cooed.

"Another?" Ada asked as she introduced another finger into Dana's ass.

"Ahhh, yes!" Dana cried out.

Ada went back to working her tongue in and around Dana's pussy as she pumped her fingers in and out of Dana's nice ass. Dana called out sharply that she was going to cum. Ada told her to cum in her mouth. When Dana was pushed over the edge she cried out to Ada to eat her cum, eat all of her cum; to suck the cum out of her sweet pink pussy; to fill her belly with her juices; to eat it, eat her cum.

"Your turn?" Dana asked when Ada climbed out from between her legs, pulling off the latex glove. Ada didn't answer. Instead she walked over to a nightstand and picked up a handkerchief to wipe the cum from her face.

"Ada?" Dana asked as she sat up on the bed, the wet from her pussy soaking the down filled comforter.

"On your hands and knees, please," Ada instructed and Dana obeyed. Dana turned her head to the side and watched with hungry eyes as Ada opened the nightstand drawer and pulled out a strap-on dildo equipped with vaginal and anal plugs for her own stimulation. Dana watched with anticipation as Ada slipped her feet into the strap-on and pulled it up to her thighs. Ada then grabbed some lubrication from the nightstand drawer and applied it generously to both the vaginal and anal plugs even though the vaginal one probably didn't need it as she was very wet from giving Dana head and fingering her pretty little asshole. Ada eased the the vaginal plug in first, pulling the strap-on up until it was snugly between her pussy lips. Ada smiled at Dana watching her and Dana smiled back. Ada then pressed the anal plug against her asshole diligently until it fell inside her with a pop. Ada sighed audibly when the anal plug finally went inside.

Ada looked down at the vulnerable Dana on her hands and knees positively waiting, and wanting her hard rubber cock inside of her. Ada looked at her for a few moments and noticed the excitement in Dana's eyes.

"Do you want me to fuck you?" Ada asked. Dana bit her lower lip and nodded her head.

"Anywhere?" Ada asked.

"Anywhere." Dana stated boldly.

Ada walked behind the subservient Dana. Resting a hand on her back she guided the cock with the other to Dana's pussy and pushed it in ever so gently. Dana cooed with electric pleasure. Ada began working the rubber dick in and out of Dana's pussy, pushing so deep she would bottom out at Dana's cervix giving a mixture of pleasure and pain to the young woman. Ada reached out and grabbed a fistful of hair and pulled Dana back against her rubber cock. Dana arched her spine and twisted back to give Ada a kiss and their tongues snaked together, the spit smearing across each others face. They fucked like that for a while. Sweat was beginning to bead upon both their bodies and Ada leaned down to lick the perspiration from Dana's back.

"I've got something else for you." Ada teased. She pulled the rubber dick out of Dana's climaxed pussy and placed the fake glans at the entrance to her sphincter. Dana oh'd and ah'd with anticipation. Ada pushed the rubber dick rubber balls deep into Dana's pliant asshole.

"You like getting fucked in the ass?" Ada asked.

"I love it!" Dana cried out.

Ada then began screwing Dana in the ass with her fake cock. Dana began calling out a mantra of 'fuck me, fuck me, fuck me' as the muscles in her ass milked and tugged on the rubber dick. And Ada obliged. She pumped into Dana's ass so fiercely that the rubber balls were smacking against Dana's pussy. Dana leaned down laying her head on the down comforter, her hands balling the fabric in her tightly clenched fists, her mouth biting the fabric until her teeth hurt.

Ada sensing the moment to be ripe plucked it and pushed down hard on Dana's shoulders and back pressing her forcefully into the down comforter, still pumping her rubber dick violently in and out of Dana's sweet, soft insides. Dana sensing her own moment told Ada to hold for a second as she slid from her knees to lay flat on her belly. Ada followed her motions and held her self up by her arms until Dana was comfortable.

"Ready?"Ada asked.

"Yes, fuck me." Dana cried out softly.

Ada fucked Dana's pink ass until it was tender and sore. Dana loved the pain and had cum so many times she lost track at twenty-three. Ada gripped Dana's shoulders for leverage as she reamed her with the rubber dick pulling her back onto the cock for all she was worth.

Dana was not alone in the climaxing. With the vaginal and anal plug gyrating inside her with every motion made her cum almost as many times as Dana had, but alas she also lost count. The vaginal plug was covered in so much juice that it was almost slipping in and out, practically fucking her. The same with the butt plug, it was almost fucking her as well being slightly pushed and pulled with the restrictions of her anal muscles.

Ada finally pulled out of Dana's asshole with a soft pop. Sweaty and shaking from her own multiple climaxes she still knelt down near Dana's gaping ass and pulled her cheeks apart and pushed her tongue into the closing orifice. She tongue fucked Dana's ass until it closed upon her stretched tongue.

"How was that?" Ada asked standing up and removing the strap-on.

"Awesome!" Dana said eyes closed and slightly delirious.

"Good, now it's my turn." And with that Ada crawled onto the bed next to Dana.

Dana leaned toward Ada and they kissed passionately for several long moments before Dana made her way to Ada's posterior, leaving a trail of butterfly kisses in her wake across Ada's body. Dana pulled Ada's ass cheeks apart exposing her own wet pussy and ass from the lubrication both natural and unnatural to Dana's feasting eyes. Dana blew cool air gently on Ada's ass before giving it the tongue fucking of her life. She pushed her tongue deep inside Ada's pink anus, and she sucked and licked feverishly at the taboo hole. Dana slid two fingers easily into Ada's very wet pussy, and following the curve of her vagina found the hard nub of her g-spot and began to press on it as hard as she could while pumping her fingers in and out. Dana ate out Ada's beautiful ass like that for sometime.

Ada's beautiful body tensed and relaxed with every orgasm she had. Dana could feel the anal muscles spasm around her tongue, which only spurred her on to make it happen again and again. Dana ate out Ada's but with great fervor, attacking the little star with a passion. She loved eating out asshole, especially a woman's, and Ada basked in her expert tongue. Ada told her to stop when she was satisfied with that aspect of their love-making. Ada then led Dana to the bathroom and began running the shower, cold. Dana was ordered inside and her nipples were instantly hard (just add cold water!). Ada climbed in after her and they washed each other, paying special attention to their pussy's and comfortably sore asses. Dana leaned low and pulled Ada's nipples into her mouth and bit them softly. Ada held Dana's head to her breast while she suckled and bit.

Dana pulled away. "Let me," she said.

Ada caught in this spider's web consented. "Anything."

"Anything?"

"Anything."

Dana squatted down in the bath. Ada instinctively tilted her pelvis forward. Dana began drinking the water pouring down her body and dripping off of her pussy like a faucet, all the while licking and lapping at Ada's swollen, erect, and protruding clitoris. Dana reached behind Ada and pulled her taut ass cheeks apart and began stroking her index finger over her sensitive anus. Ada came in Dana's mouth.

Dana stood up and turned Ada around and pressed her lithe body against the cold wall of the shower stall. Dana reached for the bullet-shaped shampoo bottle and opened it upon Ada's protruding ass pouring the slippery liquid down her crack. Dana closed the bullet-shaped shampoo bottle and pressed it against Ada's anus. Ada gasped, and then cried out sharply as the bullet penetrated her ever so gently, ever so slowly. Ada bit into her finger then her knuckles as she tried in vain to channel the pain away from her ass.

"Do you like it?" Dana asked above the din the shower was making as it hit both of their hot bodies.

"I love it! Fuck me!" Ada groaned through her knuckles as she still bit down on them. Dana snaked her hand around Ada and rubbed her stiff little clit as she twisted the bullet into Ada's ass so gently, so slowly. Ada came hard several times as Dana pushed and pulled and twisted the bullet in and out of her numbed ass.

When Ada had come down from cloud nine, the bullet slipped easily out of her ass with a push and Dana placed it back where she found it. Dana stood up and they kissed, holding each other beneath the spray of the shower until the water ran cold. They got out and dried each other off. They both walked naked through the condo.

"Help yourself to the fridge and make yourself a snack." Ada said to Dana.

"I already did," Dana said and they both laughed.

Shortly after the sexual tension came down and they were both comfortably relaxed did they dress and make their leave. Back in the Lexus they were on their way back to the café where they met. The conversation was light and they smiled at each other knowingly throughout the drive. Dana was dropped off in front of the café and she gave Ada a public kiss before she left and said her goodbyes.

Dana walked back into the café. She went to the counter and ordered a latte and a piece of bakery. The girl at the counter gave her a suggestive smile and a polite comment. Dana cleverly sat where she could see and be seen by the cute cashier whose nametag read Rian. She slyly flashed Rian her panty-less pussy several times, receiving a charming smile from the cashier every time.

"I'm taking my break now!" Rian called out a little too loudly, but purposefully. She took off her apron and walked towards the bathroom. She shot Dana a mischievous smile as she played with her hair. Then she entered the woman's bathroom.

Dana taking the hint and followed and thought to herself that yes, she was a nymphomaniac, but so what. But what's in a name? She thought. A rose by any other name would smell just as sweet. And she hoped Rian did too as the bathroom door closed behind her.

End.